A WINNING SKILLS BOOK

You Can Get Rid of Bad Habits!

Joy Berry

Illustrated by Bartholomew

Joy Berry Enterprises

Copyright © Joy Berry, 2022
Originally Published 2013

All rights are reserved.

No part of this book can be duplicated or used without the prior written permission of the copyright owner, except for the use of brief quotations from the book.

For inquiries or permission requests contact the publisher.

Published by Joy Berry Enterprises
www.joyberryenterprises.com

Joy Berry
Enterprises

You can get rid of your bad habits if you
- understand what habits are,
- learn the difference between good and bad habits,
- recognize your bad habits,
- know why you develop bad habits,
- follow the six steps for eliminating bad habits, and
- remember some things that make it easier to overcome bad habits.

WHAT HABITS ARE

A habit is something that you have done so often or for so long that you do it without thinking.

If you are like most people, you have many habits.

Some of your habits are good. Your **good habits** can benefit you and possibly the people around you.

Your good habits also can benefit the world in which you live.

Some of your habits might be bad. Your **bad habits** can annoy or harm you or the people around you.

Your bad habits also can be harmful to the world in which you live.

RECOGNIZE YOUR BAD HABITS

There are at least four ways to tell whether or not you have a bad habit.

#1: You might have a bad habit if you cannot keep yourself from doing something that you don't want to do or should not do.

#2: You might have a bad habit if you continually do something that is unpleasant and bothers other people.

#3: You might have a bad habit if you continually lie about something that you do so that no one will know that you do it.

#4: You might have a bad habit if you continually do something that makes you feel guilty.

WHY YOU DEVELOP BAD HABITS

There are many reasons why you might have a bad habit.

Ignorance might be a reason why you develop a bad habit. You might do something that is unacceptable because you do not know that you should not do it.

Peer pressure might be a reason why you develop a bad habit. You might do something that is unacceptable because one of your peers is doing it.

Carelessness might be a reason why you develop a bad habit. You might do something that is unacceptable because you do not care whether or not you do what is right.

Reacting to a problem might be a reason why you develop a bad habit. You might try to get rid of a problem by doing something that is unacceptable.

Anxiety might be a reason why you develop a bad habit. You might do something that is unacceptable to relieve the nervous energy that comes from worrying about something.

Boredom might be a reason why you develop a bad habit. You might do something that is unacceptable because you do not have anything else to do.

Feeling inferior might be a reason why you develop a bad habit. You might feel unimportant and do something that is unacceptable so that people will pay attention to you.

Feeling overwhelmed might be a reason why you develop a bad habit. You might think that you cannot handle the problem in your life, and you might react by doing something that is unacceptable.

No matter why you have a bad habit, you will be happier if you get rid of it. You can get rid of a bad habit by following these six steps::

Step 1: Admit that you have a bad habit.

Admit it to yourself.

It might also help to admit your bad habit to someone you trust.

Step 2: Realize that you need to quit.

Ask yourself these two questions:
- Why is this habit bad?
- How will I benefit if I get rid of this habit?

List your answers to these questions on a sheet of paper.

Ask some other people the same two questions:
- Why do you think that this a bad habit?
- How do you think that I will benefit if I get rid of this habit?

Again, list the answers you receive on a sheet of paper.

Step 3: Encourage yourself to quit.

Put the two lists containing the answers to your questions in a place where you will see them often.

Read both lists to yourself at the beginning of each day. Read them again at the end of the day.

Step 4: Prepare yourself to quit.

Talk to one or more people. They can be family members or friends. Tell these people that you would like to quit your bad habit. Ask them to remind you to stop if they see you start again.

Do other things to remind yourself to quit. Here are a few suggestions:
- Write notes to yourself, and put them in places where you will be sure to see them.
- Tie a string or put a Band-Aid around your finger.
- Put a sticker or a small piece of tape on your clothing or the back of your hand.
- Put a mark or write a message to yourself with a non-permanent ink pen on the back of your hand.

Step 5: Quit one day at a time.

It is not a good idea to promise yourself that you are going to quit your bad habit **forever**. This promise can seem like an impossible goal. It can discourage you and cause you to give up before you have succeeded.

Quitting one day at a time is a better goal because it is one that you can achieve.

Here is how to quit one day at a time:
- Begin each day by promising yourself that you will not give in to your bad habit for **that day**.
- With the help of your lists, other people, and your personal reminders, quit for **that day**.
- At the end of the day, think about your success and share it with another person.

The good feeling that you get from succeeding will make you want to try again the next day. If you can succeed for 21 consecutive days, your bad habit most likely will be broken.

Step 6: Replace the bad habit with a good habit.

When you finally get rid of your bad habit, you most likely will feel as though you have lost something. This may cause you to feel uncomfortable.

To avoid this "sense of loss," you need to replace the bad habit with a good habit.

It will be easier for you to get rid of a bad habit if you do these things:

Keep yourself busy so that you will not have time to think about or continue your bad habit.

Spend time with people who will encourage you. Encouragement from other people can motivate you to continue your efforts toward succeeding.

Keep track of your success by
- making a chart and putting a sticker on it for every day that you succeed or
- marking off your successful days on a calendar.

Reward yourself whenever you succeed. Do something that you like to do, or allow yourself to have something that you want at the end of a successful day. Make sure that your rewards are things that are good for you.

OVERCOMING BAD HABITS

It will be easier for you to get rid of a bad habit if you avoid doing certain things.

Do not allow yourself to think, "I can't!" Instead think positive thoughts such as:
- "I can do anything that I want to do!"
- "I can control this bad habit instead of letting it control me."

Do not allow yourself to focus on your failures. If you are not successful for a period of time, don't dwell on it. Instead, concentrate on your past successes. Also, think about succeeding in the future.

Do not allow yourself to focus on any pleasure that you might get from your bad habit. Instead, concentrate on the benefits that you will again from getting rid of the bad habit.

Do not allow yourself to make excuses for your bad habit. Inventing excuses makes it easier for you to fail. Here are some common excuses that you should avoid telling yourself:
- "No one is perfect."
- "Everyone has at least one bad habit."
- "My friend has a habit that is worse than mine."
- "It's just a little habit that doesn't really matter."
- "I don't have time to quit."
- "I'm not ready to quit today. I'll quit some other day."

It takes effort to get rid of a bad habit. It is seldom easy.

If you do not develop a bad habit, you will not have to go through the effort of overcoming it. This is why you should not do anything that might become a bad habit. Talk to the people you know. Observe them. Find out what their bad habits are. Then avoid developing the same bad habits.

A good rule to follow is this:

Do not become involved in anything that is harmful to
- you,
- other people, or
- your environment.

CONCLUSION

If you have tried your best but cannot give up a bad habit, it might be for one of two reasons.

1. Your bad habit might be an **addiction**. You might have become dependent on that habit, and you might be afraid that you will not be OK if you give it up.
2. You might have **problems** that have not been resolved. These problems might be the reason for you bad habit.

CONCLUSION

In either case, you most likely will need professional help with
- overcoming your addiction of
- solving your problems.

Getting rid of a bad habit can make you a better person, and it can enhance your life.

Therefore, the work that you put into getting rid of a bad habit will be worth it in the long run.

www.ingramcontent.com/pod-product-compliance
Lightning Source LLC
Chambersburg PA
CBHW081408070526
44583CB00020B/2731